BEDŘICH SMETANA

MÁ VLAST
MEIN VATERLAND

No. 6 Blaník
Symphonic Poem
Sinfonische Dichtung

Ernst Eulenburg Ltd

London · Mainz · Madrid · New York · Paris · Tokyo · Toronto · Zürich

BEDŘICH SMETANA
Má Vlast

During the years 1858–61, while he was in Sweden and strongly under Liszt's influence, Smetana composed three symphonic poems based on dramas by Shakespeare (*Richard III*), Schiller (*Wallenstein's Camp*) and Öhlenschläger (*Haakon Jarl*). Up to that time these were his most important symphonic works. More than a decade later, on 27 June 1873, an article appeared in the Czech musical periodical *Dalibor*, in which V. J. Novotný stated that Smetana was planning to write a series of symphonic poems on subjects which had strong associations with episodes in Czech history and legend, and that he was intending to include 'Vyšehrad', 'Vltava', 'Říp', 'Lipany' and 'Bílá Hora' (the White Mountain) in his cycle. The general title of the work was to be *Vlast* (The Fatherland). Smetana had been considering this project for several months, and is believed to have begun sketching the first of the new series of symphonic poems before he completed his fourth opera, *Libuše,* on 12 November 1872. This epic festival opera is concerned with the founding of the first Czech dynasty, and concludes with Libuše's visions of the heroes and leaders of her nation and her prophesies of the glorious future they would bring to her land and her people. It is therefore clear that Smetana conceived his cycle of symphonic poems as a monumental orchestral work which would be complementary to *Libuše* and would present and emphasize aspects of his nation's history which he was unable to cover in his opera. The first symphonic poem, *Vyšehrad*, is very closely linked with *Libuše*, both thematically and also in its general character. It is primarily concerned with prophesies of the nation's future by seers in the historic fortress of Prague (Vyšehrad), where Libuše reigned with her consort.

During the years in which this ambitious scheme came to fruition (1872–9), details of the plan were altered. Smetana substituted four new subjects in place of 'Říp', 'Lipany' and 'Bílá Hora', and the title was changed to *Má vlast* (My Fatherland). Two of the symphonic poems (*Vltava* and *From Bohemia's Fields and Forests*) represent features of the Czech countryside, but also refer to the life of the people; *Šárka* is a concise drama based on the legend of a Czech amazon; aspects of the Hussite wars are dealt with in the last two tone poems (*Tábor* and *Blaník*), the second of which envisages the resurrection and final victory of the nation. The composer helped to give his cycle a musical unity by concluding *Vltava* and *Blaník* with the Vyšehrad motifs, which in turn stem from his opera *Libuše*. Furthermore, *Tábor* and *Blaník* are each based musically on the same celebrated Hussite chorale, and the one is in reality a continuation of the other.

It is easy to overlook the fact that these six symphonic poems were completed during a most unhappy period of Smetana's life. The first four were composed when he was being reviled by the critics and while he was vainly seeking for a cure for his total deafness. The last two were written when he had become resigned to his fate, but while he was still being shabbily treated by the

Theatre Association. Nevertheless he found solace in composing these national compositions, which breathe such a remarkably optimistic spirit. He had the satisfaction of witnessing the very successful first performance of the entire cycle conducted by Adolf Čech on 5 November 1882.

Blaník

After John Hus was treacherously burnt at the stake early in the 15th century, the Táborites, led by Žižka, rose in revolt against the powerful and corrupt Church of Rome and the Germanic domination of their land. They carried all before them until 1436, when they were finally crushed by their rivals, the Utraquists, whom the Church had been forced to recognize temporarily. Tábor, fifty miles south of Prague, was the stronghold of Žižka's puritan army.

The fifth and sixth symphonic poems, *Tábor* and *Blaník*, turn to the Hussite wars for their inspiration, and hence they form a direct link with Libuše's prophesies in Smetana's festival opera. In that work a brief reminder of the Hussite period among the series of visions of the high points of Bohemian history could hardly serve to emphasize its significance adequately from the standpoint of Czech nationalism. In the nineteenth century these wars were primarily viewed as an assertion of national rights, and their religious aspect was minimized. They were regarded as the most momentous and decisive of the struggles against outside forces, on the outcome of which ultimate supremacy and freedom of the Czech peoples hung in the balance. Consequently after due consideration – an interval of three years separates *From Bohemia's Fields and Groves* from *Tábor* – Smetana became fully conscious of the need to present the Hussite period in a truer perspective, and so he completed *Má vlast* with two large scale works devoted to this subject.

Smetana gave the following description of *Blaník* in the *Short Outline of the Contents of the Symphonic Poems* which he sent to his publisher F. A. Urbánek at the end of May 1879:

> This is a continuation of the preceding work, *Tábor*. After their defeat the Hussite heroes took refuge *in Blaník* [mountain] and waited in a deep slumber for the time when their country had need of them. So in *Blaník*, just as in *Tábor*, those same motifs from 'Ye who are God's warriors!' form the foundation of the structure. On the basis of *this melody* (of this Hussite principle) will develop *the resurrection* and *the future happiness and glory of the Czech nation!* In the form of a march this victorious hymn brings the composition to an end, and thus it also concludes the

whole cycle of symphonic poems, 'The Fatherland'. There is in addition
a short idyll in this work, like a little intermezzo, a sketch of the situation
of Blaník: a young shepherd boy shouts and plays (a shawm), and he is
answered by an echo.

With this description of Smetana's last symphonic poem before us,
it becomes clear that the work falls into the following five sections:
I. The defeated Hussite warriors retreat into their mountain refuge
(*Allegro moderato*, bars 1–69);
II. Pastoral interlude (*Andante non troppo – Più allegro, ma non molto*,
bars 70–138);
III. The distress and suffering of the people (*Più mosso – Meno mosso*,
bars 139–229);
IV. The Hussites emerge and restore peace to their land (*Tempo di
marcia – Grandioso – Tempo I – Più vivo* (bars 230–388);
V. Glory returns to Bohemia (*Largamente maestoso – Largamente
grandioso, Meno allegro – Vivace*, bars 389–441).

The work opens with direct references to the initial bar of the chorale
'Ye who are God's warriors' (a) and to the distinctive three-note
figure from the chorale's second bar (b).

The collapse of stable tonality at bar 4 appears to suggest the failure
of the Hussites. The warriors proceed to Blaník to a theme derived
from the beginning of this Dorian chorale melody (bars 15ff.). It
will be noticed that in bars 17–18, 24–25, 32–33 and elsewhere the
three-note figure gives rise to characteristic Moravian modulations,
that is, modulations from a minor key to the major key whose tonic
lies one tone lower. As we are aware, Smetana favoured thematic
cross-reference, even in circumstances in which it would be wrong
to expect similarities of poetic implication or of mood. A result of
this is greater unification than would otherwise have been possible.
In the present work the three-note figure (b) forms the basis of one

of the idyllic episode's themes (bars 78–80), a theme which reappears in the turbulent *Più mosso* (bars 145–146), and re-emerges again later (bars 214–217 and 271–274). (b) occurs inverted in the *Più mosso* (1st violins, bars 142–144), and even the theme in triplets in the *Meno mosso* (bars 165ff.) apparently stems from the same pithy musical germ. A new theme, anticipated by a horn and by trombones in bars 218–221 and 224–227, forms the basis of the fourth section of the symphonic poem, and gives an impression of the Hussites responding to the call of their country. It takes the form of a march and grows directly out of the last phrase of 'Ye who are God's warriors', but avoids the minor mode of the chorale and breathes a spirit of confidence in the key of F major (*Tempo di marcia*, bars 230ff.). On reaching the key of D major it is restated triumphantly by the full orchestra (*Grandioso*, bars 287ff.). After a quiet interlude it returns again richly scored (*Tempo I*, bars 362ff.), but this time an increase of speed transforms it into a polka (*Più vivo*, bars 370ff.).

The climax is reached in the coda. Here the opening phrase of the Hussite chorale for trumpets and trombones is combined with the stately Vyšehrad motif for woodwind and strings (*Largamente maestoso*, bars 389ff.), and shortly afterwards, while the trumpets reaffirm the Vyšehrad motif, the piccolo and 1st violins, supported by the rest of the woodwind and strings, superimpose the Vyšehrad's second, fanfare-like motif (*Largamente grandioso. Meno allegro*, bars 398–400). In the *Vivace* the main Vyšehrad motif is heard once more on the trumpets (bars 417–424). By reintroducing the two themes from his first symphonic poem, Smetana emphasized the inherant cyclic nature of *Má vlast*. When the composer wrote to Hostinský on 9 January, 1879, he pointed out that he had used the last phrase of the Hussite chorale deliberately in order to end *Blaník* and indeed the whole cycle triumphantly, for the chorale verse ends with these words: 'So that finally with Him you will always be victorious'.

Smetana composed *Blaník* directly after *Tábor* and completed the full score on 9 March 1879. He finished his piano duet arrangement of the work on 4 April that year. *Tábor* and *Blaník* were both given their first performances under Adolf Čech's direction on 4 January 1880, at a concert in Prague commemorating the 50th anniversary of the composer's first appearance as a solo pianist at the age of six, at a concert of the Philosophical Academy at his birthplace, Litomyšl.

F. A. Urbánek published the piano duet version of *Blaník* on 6 July 1880, and issued the full score posthumously on 2 August 1894. Among other compositions in which the chorale 'Ye who are God's warriors' appears may be mentioned Liszt's *Hussitenlied* for piano duet (1840), Dvořák's *Hussite* Overture, op. 67 (1883), Suk's symphonic poem *Prague,* op. 26 (1904), and Janáček's opera *Mr. Brouček's Excursion to the 15th Century* (1917).

John Clapham.

This score was revised in 1975 when many small errors were eliminated.

BEDŘICH SMETANA
Má Vlast

Während der Jahre 1858–61, die Smetana in Schweden verbrachte, und als er noch sehr unter Liszts Einfluss stand, komponierte er drei sinfonische Dichtungen, denen Dramen von Shakespeare (*Richard III*), Schiller (*Wallensteins Lager*) und Öhlenschläger (*Haakon Jarl*) zugrunde lagen. Es waren die bedeutendsten sinfonischen Werke, die er bisher geschrieben hatte. Über zehn Jahre später, am 27. Juni 1873, erschien ein Artikel in der tschechischen Musikzeitschrift *Dalibor*, in dem V. J. Novotný erklärte, dass Smetana sich mit dem Gedanken trug, einen Zyklus sinfonischer Dichtungen über Themen zu schreiben, die eng mit der tschechischen Geschichte und den Legenden des Landes, darunter „Vyšehrad", „Vltava", Říp, „Lipany" und Bilá Hora' (der weisse Berg) verbunden waren. Das Werk sollte den Gesamttitel *Vlast* (das Vaterland) tragen. Mit diesem Plan hatte sich Smetana damals schon einige Monate beschäftigt, und man nimmt an, dass er damit begann, die erste in der Reihe der sinfonischen Dichtungen zu skizzieren, bevor er noch (am 12. November 1872) seine vierte Oper, *Libuše*, vollendet hatte. Diese epische Festspieloper handelt von der Gründung der ersten tschechischen Dynastie. Sie schliesst mit der Vision Libuševs, in der ihr die Helden und Führer ihrer Nation erscheinen, von denen sie weissagt, dass ihrem Land und Volk durch sie eine glorreiche Zukunft beschieden sei. Daraus ergibt sich, dass Smetana sich seinen Zyklus sinfonischer Dichtungen als ein monumentales Orchesterwerk vorgestellt hat, das seine Oper ergänzen und jene Momente in der Geschichte seines Volks behandeln und hervorheben sollte, die er in der Oper nicht hatte berücksichtigen können. Die erste sinfonische Dichtung, *Vyšehrad,* hat mit dieser Oper, was Themen und Wesensart anbelangt, vieles gemeinsam. Sie handelt hauptsächlich von den Prophezeiungen der Weissager über die Zukunft der Nation und spielt sich in der historischen Prager Festung (Vyšehrad) ab, in welcher Libuše mit ihrem Gemahl die Herrschaft führte.

Während der Jahre, in denen dieser grossangelegte Plan entwickelt und verwirklicht wurde (1872–79), wurden im Entwurf verschiedene Einzelheiten geändert. So ersetzte Smetana „Říp", „Lipany" und Bilá Hora' durch den Stoff vier neuer Themen. Auch der Gesamttitel wurde geändert und lautete nun *Má Vlast* (Mein Vaterland). Zwei der sinfonischen Dichtungen (*Vltava* und *Aus Böhmens Wiesen und Wäldern*) haben die tschechische Landschaft als Thema, beziehen sich aber auch auf das Leben der Leute; *Šárka* ist ein kurzgefasstes Drama, das auf der Legende einer tschechische Amazone beruht; Die Hussitenkriege werden in den letzten beiden Tondichtungen (*Tábor* und *Blaník*) behandelt, von denen die letztere die Auferstehung und den endgültigen Sieg der Nation verkündet. Die musikalische Einheit des Zyklus wurde vom Komponisten dadurch gefördert, dass er *Vltava* und *Blaník* mit den beiden Vyšehradmotiven beschloss, die ihrerseits aus seiner Oper *Libuše* stammen. Weiterhin beruhen sowohl *Tábor* wir *Blaník* auf dem selben berühmten Hussitenchoral, und die letztere Tondichtung, ist in Wirklichkeit als eine Fortsetzung der ersteren anzusehen.

Man ist leicht dazu veranlasst, die Tatsache zu übersehen, dass diese sechs sinfonischen Dichtungen zu einer Zeit vollendet wurden, als Smetana besonders unglücklich war. Während der Komposition der ersten vier, wurde er von den Kritikern geschmäht; auch suchte er damals vergebens nach einer Heilung füs seine völlige Taubheit. Die beiden letzten wurden zwar geschrieben, als er sich schon mit seinem Schicksal abgefunden hatte, doch wurde er zu der Zeit von der Theatergenossenschaft immer noch schändlich behandelt. Allerdings fand er Trost beim Komponieren dieser patriotischen Werke, die von einem so auffallend zuversichtlichen Geist beseelt sind. Am 5. November 1882 hatte er dann auch die Genugtuung, der ersten höchst erfolgreichen Aufführung des ganzen Zyklus, unter der Leitung von Adolf Čech, beizuwohnen.

Blaník

Als Johannes Hus zu Anfang des 15. Jahrhunderts durch Verrat seinen Tod auf dem Scheiterhaufen fand, erhoben sich die Taboriten unter Žižka gegen die mächtige und korrupte römische Kirche, sowie gegen die deutsche Herrschaft über ihr Land. Bis 1436 konnten sie sich behaupten, aber dann wurden sie durch ihre Gegner, die Utraquisten, zu deren Anerkennung die Kirche eine Beitlang gezwungen war, endgültig vernichtet. Die 80 km südlich von Prag liegende Feste Tábor war die Hochburg des puritanischen Heeres unter Žižka.

Die fünfte und sechse der sinfonischen Dichtungen, *Tábor* und *Blaník,* sind von den Hussitenkriegen inspiriert worden und stehen daher eng mit den Weissagungen Libušes aus Smetanas Festspieloper in Verbindung. Vom Standpunkt des tschechischen Nationalismus aus leuchtet es ein, dass die blosse Einbeziehung der Hussitenzeit in die Reihe der Visionen, welche die Höhepunkte der böhmischen Geschichte darstellen, allein kaum ihre Bedeutung genügend hervorheben könnte, denn im neunzehnten Jahrhundert wurde sie nicht so sehr als ein Religionskonflikt, sondern vielmehr als eine Verteidigung nationaler Rechte angesehen. Man hielt sie für die Zeit der folgenschwersten und entscheidendsten Kämpfe gegen die ausländischen Mächte, von deren Ausgang die endgültige Oberhoheit und die Freiheit des tschechischen Volkes abhängig war. Aus diesem Grunde, und nach reiflicher Überlegung – drei Jahre liegen zwischen den Kompositionen *Aus Böhmens Hain und Flur* und *Tábor* – war sich Smetana durchaus bewusst, dass man den Geist der Hussitenzeit getreuer wiedergeben müsste, weshalb er dann *Má vlast* mit zwei grossangelegten Werken über dieses Thema abschloss.

In seinem *Kurzen Abriss des Inhalts der sinfonischen Dichtungen,* den er Ende Mai 1879 an seinen Verleger F. A. Urbánek schickte, beschrieb Smetana *Blaník* mit den folgenden Worten:

> Dies ist eine Fortsetzung des vorhergehenden Werks *Tábor.* Nach ihrer Niederlage nahmen die Helden der Hussiten Zuflucht *im* [Berg] *Blaník* und warteten in tiefem Schlaf auf den Augenblick in dem sie ihrem Land zu Hilfe kommen sollten. Daher bilden in *Blaník,* wie in *Tábor* dieselben Motive aus „Ihr, die Gottes Streiter seid!", das Fundament der Struktur. Auf *dieser Melodie* (diesem hussitischen Prinzip) basierend, wird sich die *Auferstehung* und *das zukünftige Glück und die Glorie der tschechischen Nation* entwickeln! In der Form eines Marsches führt dieser siegreiche Choral die Komposition zum Abschluss und beschliesst damit auch den ganzen Zyklus „Das Vaterland". Ausserdem enthält das Werk ein kurzes Idyll, wie ein kleines Intermezzo, eine Skizze der Lage des Berges Blaník: ein Schäferjunge ruft und spielt (eine Schalmei), und ein Echo antwortet ihm.

Aus dieser Beschreibung der vorliegenden letzten sinfonischen Dichtung Smetanas, ergibt es sich deutlich, dass das Werk in die folgenden fünf Abschnitte zerfällt:

I Die geschlagenen Krieger der Hussiten ziehen sich in ihre Zuflucht in den Bergen zurück (*Allegro moderato,* Takt 1–69);

II Ländliches Zwischenspiel (*Andante non troppo- Più allegro, ma non molto,* Takt 70–138);

III Verzweiflung und Leiden des Volkes (*Più mosso – Meno mosso,* Takt 139–229);

IV Die Hussiten erheben sich und bringen ihrem Land wieder Frieden (*Tempo di marcia – Grandioso – Tempo I – Più vivo* (Takt 230–388);

V Böhmen wird wieder glorreich (*Largamente maestoso – Largamente grandioso, Meno allegro – Vivace,* Takt 389–441).

Gleich am Anfang bezieht sich das Werk unmittelbar auf den ersten Takt des Chorals „Ihr, die Gottes Streiter seid" (a), und auf die charakteristische, aus drei Noten bestehende Figur in zweiten Takt des Chorals (b).

Der Zusammenbruch der stabilen Tonalität im vierten Takt, mag auf den Fehlschlag der Hussiten hindeuten. Von einem Thema begleitet, das dem Anfang der dorischen Choralmelodie entstammt (Takt 15ff.), begeben sich die Krieger zum Blaník. Es wäre zu bemerken, dass die aus drei Noten bestehende Figur in den Takten 17-18, 24-25, 32-33, und auch an anderen Stellen, typisch mährische Modulationen verursacht, d.h., Modulationen von einer Moll- zu der Durtonart, deren Grundton eine Stufe tiefer steht. Wie bekannt, hat Smetana eine Vorliebe für Verweisungen von einem Thema zum anderen auch in Fällen gehabt, in denen es verfehlt wäre, Ähnlichkeiten in der poetischen Bedeutung oder in der Stimmung vorauszusetzen. Das hat zur Folge, dass dadurch eine grössere Einheitlichkeit entsteht, als sonst möglich wäre. Im vorliegenden Werk bildet die aus drei Noten bestehende Figur (b) die Basis für eines der Themen in der idyllischen Episode (Takt 78-80), und dieses Thema tritt ebenso in dem stürmischen *Più mosso* (Takt 145-146), und auch später wieder auf (Takt 214-217 und 271-274). Im *Più mosso* steht (b) in der Umkehrung (erste Geigen Takt 142-144), und selbst das Triolenthema im *Meno mosso* (Takt 165ff.), scheint aus derselben kraftvollen Keimzelle hervorgegangen zu sein. Ein neues Thema, von einem Horn und den Posaunen in Takt 218-221 und 224-227 vorweggenommen, bildet die Basis für den vierten Abschnitt der sinfonischen Dichtung und stellt die Hussiten dar, die dem Ruf ihres Landes folgen. Es hat die Form eines Marsches und ist unmittelbar aus dem letzten Teil des Chorals, „Ihr, die Gottes Streiter seid", entstanden, vermeidet aber die Molltonart des Chorals und strömt in F-Dur den Geist der Zuversicht aus (*Tempo di marcia*, Takt 230ff.). In D-Dur wird es dann triumphierend vom ganzen Orchester wiederholt (*Grandioso*, Takt 287ff.). Nach einem Zwischenspiel in ruhigerer Stimmung taucht es wieder in reicher Instrumentierung auf (*Tempo I*, Takt 362ff.), doch wird es diesmal durch eine Beschleunigung des Tempos in eine Polka umgewandelt (*Più vivo*, Takt 370ff.)

Der Höhepunkt wird in der Koda erreicht. Hier wird der Anfang des Hussitenchorals, für Trompeten und Posaunen gesetzt, mit dem erhabenen, von Holzbläsern und Streichern gespielten Vyšehradmotiv vereint (*Largamente maestoso*, Takt 389ff.), und kurz darauf, während die Trompeten das Vyšehradmotiv nochmals bestätigen, erklingt darüber, von Piccolo und ersten Geigen gespielt und von den übrigen Holzbläsern und Streichern begleitet, das zweite, fanfarenartige Vyšehradmotiv (*Largamente grandioso. Meno allegro*, Takt 398-400).

Im *Vivace* tritt dann das Vyšehradhauptmotiv noch einmal in den Trompetenstimmen auf (Takt 417–424). Durch die Einführung der beiden Themen aus der ersten sinfonischen Dichtung hat Smetana die zyklische Einheit des Gesamtwerks *Má vlast* betont. Als der Komponist am 9. Januar 1879 an Kostinský schrieb, wies er darauf hin, dass er den letzten Teil des Hussitenchorals durchaus bewusst verwendet hat, um damit *Blaník*, und zugleich den ganzen Zyklus, triumphal abzuschliessen, denn der Choral endet mit den Worten: „Dass ihr am Ende mit Ihm immer siegreich bleibt".

Smetana hat *Blaník* gleich nach *Tábor* komponiert. Die Partitur hat er am 9. März 1879 vollendet. Das Arrangement des Werks für Klavier zu vier Händen wurde am 4. April desselben Jahres fertig. *Tábor* und *Blaník* wurden zusammen am 4. Januar 1880 in Prag unter der Leitung von Adolf Čech uraufgeführt. Der Anlass dazu war der fünfzigste Jahrestag eines Konzerts, bei dem der damals sechsjährige Komponist erstmalig als Solopianist auftrat, und das von der philosophischen Akadamie in seinem Geburtsort, Litomyšl, gegeben wurde. F. A. Urbánek veröffentlichte das vierhändige Arrangement von *Blaník* am 6. Juli 1880, und gab die Partitur am 2. August 1894, nach Smetanas Tod heraus. Unter den anderen Werken, in denen der Choral „Ihr, die Gottes Streiter seid" verwendet wurde, mögen hier Liszts *Hussitenlied* für Klavier zu vier Händen (1840), Dvořáks *Hussitenovertüre, Op. 67* (1883), Suks sinfonische Dichtung *Prag, Op. 26* (1904) und Janáčeks Oper *Ausflug des Herrn Brouček ins 15. Jahrhundert* (1917) erwähnt werden.

John Clapham
Deutsche Übersetzung Stefan de Haan

Die vorliegende Partitur wurde 1975 revidiert, wobei viele geringfügige Fehler korrigiert wurden.

Blaník

Allegro moderato. ♩ = 72.

B. Smetana
1824-1884

E. E. 3646

Ernst Eulenburg Ltd

2

E. E. 3646

4

8

9

Più Allegro ma non molto. ♩ = 76.

18

123

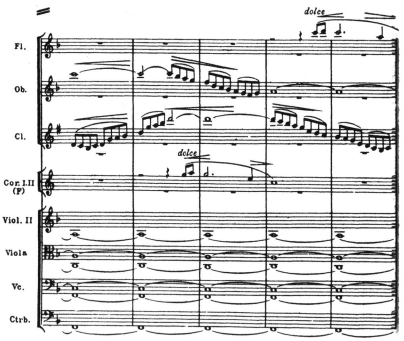

28

187

muta in C F

208

230 Tempo di marcia. ♩ = 92.

48

54   277

63

E.E.3646

68

362

Tempo I.

69

E.E. 8646

Più vivo.

375

383

ritard.

Largamente maestoso.

E.E.3646

E. E. 3646

E.E. 3646

E. E. 3646